Self-Esteem

Building

How to live your life as

YOU

Mykim Tran

Contents

Dedication

This book is dedicated to anyone who is tired of always trying to impress others to get their approval to try to fit in. It is dedicated to anyone who wants to feel good about themselves, and to anyone who wants to tap into their inner strength and talent to create their own lifestyle. Lastly, it is dedicated to anyone who wants to find true happiness within themselves.

Introduction

As human beings, our main goal is to seek for happiness. For me, I believe that happiness is based on how high your inner strength and courage levels are. The fastest way to increase your inner strength and courage is through taking action. The more action you take, the more strength and courage you will gain, the happier you will become. In order for you to have the ability to take action, you have to believe in yourself and know that you already have the strength and talent to become successful. I believe that the only way for your strength and talent to manifest is when you are being yourself. And that is why having a high self-esteem level is important.

High self-esteem is having the ability to value and believe in yourself so that you can realize that you already have enough strength and talent within you to accomplish whatever you desire. High self-esteem not only gives you the ability to accomplish things quicker and better, but it will also give you the ability to block out external influences so you can make your own decisions on what bring you happiness.

However, the moment that you allow external factors to influence you; it will become very difficult to take your identity back from others to yourself, because the influences are already within you. In this case, you want to make sure you do not give any external factor a chance to influence you at any moment. And this is what this book will help you accomplish.

This book will provide you with simple methods on how you can be yourself in order to tap into and unleash your inner strength and talent so you can create and live the lifestyle you love. You will learn how to stay strong when others are denying or trying to change you. You will learn how to use your inner strength to say "no" to other people, and learn how to block out external influences so you can make your own decision. Learn how to spot out the positive and negative people in your life.

You will be able to understand that you are still a terrific person no matter what kind of negative qualities you have or how many negative experiences you have encountered in your life. You will learn to realize that your negative qualities help build your positive qualities that will help you become a unique person. You will be able to take advantage and turn your negative qualities and experiences into opportunities. You will also discover the many more benefits that come along of having a high level of self-esteem

Your truly,

Mykim Tran

Section 1: Be Yourself

Self-Acceptance

"Happiness is really a deep harmonious inner satisfaction and approval."

Francis Wilshire

(Author of "You")

Do you believe that having few or no negative qualities will increase your self-esteem and happiness? Or have you ever tried to get rid of your negative qualities because you think that you will become a happier person?

Even though you only want to have positive qualities, you will encounter a lot of suffering if you do not accept your negative qualities because they are a part of you.

When something is already a part of you, it is difficult to change or get rid of it. When you want to change something that cannot be done, you will encounter a lot of suffering.

Did you know that everything in life, include human beings, there is always two sides to everything. For example, the color black cannot exist without the color white. A left side cannot exist without a right side. In this case, you cannot have positive qualities without negative qualities. So if you want to keep your positive qualities, you have to accept your negative qualities. If the term positive exists, then the term negative has to exist. You cannot have one without the other. If you try to delete one, the other will also be deleted.

As a human being, you cannot be perfect, which means you have to have negative qualities. It does not matter what you do, you will always have some kind of negative quality. For example, if you are able to get rid one of your negative qualities, some other negative quality will manifest in place the old one.

In this case, the only way for you to have a high level of self-esteem is through self-acceptance. Self-acceptance means accepting whom you are completely from the inside and out, both positive and negative.

However, a great thing about being a human being is that you have the ability to label which things are negative and positive. Negative and positive are just terms that are being labeled on things and people, but the true meaning all depend on you. When you label something positive, that means something else has to be labeled negative. When you label some of your qualities as negative, it does not necessarily mean that they are bad.

If you have trouble building your self-acceptance level, then try applying the following action steps:

ACTION STEPS

1. Discover as much about yourself as possible through self-development and human development by doing the following things:

   o   Read books and articles

- o   Attend workshops and seminars

- o   Listen and watch CD/DVDs

2. Pay attention how the knowledge help you understand who you are as a person

   - o   Pay attention to your likes and dislikes

   - o   Pay attention to your positive and negative qualities

   - o   Pay attention to your strengths, talents and weaknesses

The more you understand about yourself, the sooner you will understand and accept that you need both positive and negative qualities in order for you to be yourself that will translate into a high level of self-esteem. Self-development is important because it will help you build certain positive qualities that need more time than other qualities. In addition, you can never learn everything about yourself, which means that self-development should be an ongoing learning process.

Disadvantages of Not Being YOU

"To be yourself in a world that is constantly trying to make you something else is the greatest accomplishment."

Ralph Waldo Emerson

(Author of "Self-Reliance")

Have you ever thought to yourself that you would be a lot happier if you could become someone else or just have one or two of other people's positive qualities? However, when you want to become someone else or have another person positive quality, then it means that you are not giving yourself enough credit about how great a person you are. If you know and understand what kind of positive qualities you have, you would not want to become anyone else, but only want to be you. In addition, when you try to become someone else, you will encounter many disadvantages.

1st disadvantage: Loss of Freedom

Freedom means you are able to think, speak, and do whatever you desire, whenever it fits you. However, if you are trying to become someone else, then you are not in the state of freedom anymore because you are doing things that are not a part of you.

2nd disadvantage: Wasted More Time and Energy

You will realize that when you are not being yourself, you will use more time and energy just by trying to come up with different ways to speak and do things. However, when you are being you, you will spend less time and energy because what you do and say just comes out naturally. Also, you will have more time and energy to do other things that are more important to you than spending time trying to become someone else.

"Why try and to be fake when being real takes less effort."

Inspirational Quotes

(An inspirational quotes website)

3rd disadvantage: Your Positive Qualities Cannot Grow

The only way for your positive qualities to shine out to show you how great a person you are is when you are being you. When you are trying to be someone else, your body and mind will use most of their energy and time to try to accomplish what you are chasing after and not on building your positive qualities.

"It is better to be hated for what you are than to be loved for what you are not."

Andre Gide

(Author of "Passages")

If you believe that becoming someone else is better than being you, then try applying the following action steps:

ACTION STEPS

1. Write down all of your positive qualities; even the smallest ones
2. For each positive quality, write down at least five ways how your positive qualities make you a better person
3. For each positive quality, come up with at least two ways on how you can apply and make it stronger

"Concentrate on your strengths instead of your weaknesses, on your powers instead on your problems."

Paul J. Meyer

(Author of "Forgiveness Ultimate Miracle")

Dare to Be Different

"Why are you trying so hard to fit in when you were born to stand out?"

Fitness Motivator

(a website to help you be and stay fit)

Have you ever met people who are great at what they do, and then, you find yourself wanting to become like them? When you try to copy other people, you cannot seem to reach the same level of success as they are. After you failed the first time, you would try to copy another person, and then, you end up failing again. After many times of trying to copy other people and failed, you will start to believe that you are not as smart enough to become successful like other people that you idolize as. As a result, you settle for just being an average person, which prevents you to have the ability to do great things.

If you have trouble doing great things or not going toward the direction of success that you would like, then it means you are not using your own strength and talent. If that happens, it could be that you have been influenced by your family and the media to believe that you need to become like other people. For example, every time your parents see other people who are great at what they do, your parents would tell you to become like them. Also, whenever you step into society, the media put tremendous pressure on you to become like other people or things. You would most likely see advertisements trying to influence you to buy this and that to become someone else. However, you are unlikely to see advertisements that motivate and inspire you to be you.

The more you are influenced by your parents and the media, the more that your strength and talent will start to fade away. In order for your strength and talent to grow, you have to use them. However, you did not have many opportunities to use your strength and talent when you were influenced by your parents and the media. When it gets to a point that your strength and talent become weak, you will begin to believe that you do not have any strength and talent within you. As a result, you believe that in order to become successful, you have to find the strength and talent from the outside, which is to copy other people.

To tell you the truth, you will never reach the same level of greatness as other people when you try to copy them. Since each human being is gifted with different strength and talent, it means each of us is meant to accomplish different great things. If everyone is meant to accomplish the same great things, then we would all have the same strength and talent, but in this case, we don't.

If you want to accomplish great things, you have to use your own strength and talent. When you are using your own strength and talent, they will become natural to make them easy to use to help you become successful. The main reason why other people are great at what they do is because they are using their own strength and talent. However, if other people were to use your strength and talent, then they will not be as great. Even though you might not be able to accomplish the same great things as other people when you use your own strength and talent, you will still be able to reach the same level of greatness as other people.

"Always remember that you are absolutely unique. Just like everyone else."

Margaret Mead

(Author of "Growing Up in New Guinea")

"You have something to offer this world that nobody else does! You have incredible talents and gifts to share with others."

Joel Osteen

(Author of "Become a Better You")

If you have trouble discovering your own strength and talent, then try applying the following action steps:

ACTION STEPS

1. Write down all your accomplishments and successes, both small and large

2. For each accomplishment/success, write down all the strength, knowledge, skill, and talent that you have developed and gained

3. Write down every single thing that you want to accomplish

Do not limit yourself on what you want to accomplish. If you desire to accomplish something, then you already have the strength and talent to achieve it within you. Otherwise, the thought would not manifest in your mind. Sometimes the strength and talent that you will need will not unleash until you do something that requires them to develop and grow.

4. After you achieved something, write down every single strength and talent that you have developed and gained

As you accomplish more and more things, you will soon discover what your unique strength and talent are by looking at your accomplishments and successes.

"Always be a first-rate version of yourself, instead of a second-rate version of somebody else."

Judy Garland

(Hollywood's movie star, "The Wizard of Oz" and "The Judy Garland Show")

Share From Your Heart

Do you wish other people would understand you better? Do you feel that if other people understand you better, then you would have better relationships with them? If you ever encountered with these kinds of situations, then it is your responsibility to make sure that people understand you better and not the other way around. The main reason why other people might not understand you is because you did not share enough on what is important to you.

If you want other people to understand you, the fastest way is for you to share from your heart. If you have been sharing a lot to other people, but they still do not understand you, then you have not been sharing from your heart. It does not matter how much you share, people will not understand you unless you share from your heart. Also, you will began to realize that you do not need to share as much for people to understand you if you share from your heart.

If you have difficulty sharing from your heart, then there are two main reasons why. First, you believe that people might not accept and appreciate you when you share from your heart. When you share from your heart, your information will become unique. When people hear unique or uncommon things, they are less likely to accept or be attracted to you at the beginning because the attraction usually began from the similarities that you may have. When people do not accept or appreciate you, you will feel uncomfortable. As a result, sometimes you may not want to share from your heart because you fear that other people will not accept you.

The second reason is because you are living in a society that does not support deep sharing. When you share from your heart, emotions will develop that will make the situation uncomfortable. And then your parents would tell you to keep your feelings inside because they do not want to feel uncomfortable. Also, you have probably often heard the phrase, "Be a man." You have been taught that men should be tough from the outside and inside. You believe that being tough inside means not showing emotions. Living in today society, you have also been taught that it is better to be a tough person, rather than a weak person, which would means that you have to keep your emotions inside.

When you reach adulthood, it is difficult for you to share from your heart. Whenever you get a chance to share from your heart, your emotions will develop that might influence you to stop from sharing because you do not want other people to see you as a weak person. As a result, other people will never get the chance to understand who you are. The worst thing is that you never allow yourself to know what is important to you because you never let yourself express it out.

However, emotions are powerful cues that will assist in telling other people and yourself that what you share is important to you. The more emotional you get when you share something, the more important that thing is to you.

"Never apologize for showing feeling. When you do so, you apologize the truth."

Benjamin Disraeli

(Author of "Endymion")

In order to become comfortable in sharing from your heart, it is also a learning process. The beginning is always the hardest because you may get really emotional, which many cause you to feel tempted to quit sharing. However, as you keep on practicing sharing, it will get easier and your emotional level will decrease. And then, it will become a natural thing to you to share from your heart. Soon you will realize that people will understand you so well that you will have great relationships with them. As human beings, everyone wants to be connected to other people who remain true to their hearts.

If you have a difficult time sharing from your heart, then try applying the following action steps:

ACTION STEP

1. Research places that allow deep sharing

There are many support or therapy groups that support deep sharing without judgment. There are many retreat centers that hold life sharing groups. It is all about the environment. If the environment is positive, you will become positive. If the environment allows deep sharing, you will start to share from your heart without realizing it. However, if you live in an environment that does not support deep sharing, it does not matter how much you want to share from your heart, it will be difficult for you to do so.

2. Attend to these kinds of sharing environments as much as possible to help you build the habit to feel comfortable sharing from your heart.

Take Good Care of Yourself

"You make the world a better place by making yourself a better person."

Scott Sorrell

(A professional speaker)

Let me ask you this, if you really care and love someone, would you do any harm to him or her? For example, if you have a child who you love, do you harm him or her in anyway? Of course not, right? As a matter of fact, you would do whatever it takes to make sure your child is well taken care of.

The same goes for loving yourself. If you care and love yourself, you would not do anything to harm yourself in anyway; this includes physically, mentally, spiritually, emotionally, or any other way. For example, if you care and love your body, you would not consume junk foods because you know that those foods will harm your body. When you give the excuse because junk foods taste good, then that means you care less of your body than the taste of the junk foods. When you say you care about your body, but then consume junk foods, then you are contradicting yourself.

Another example would be taking care of your mind. You want to make sure to stay away from anything or anyone who could influence your mind in a negative way. For example, if you know that negative people will influence your mind in a negative way, then you should take care of yourself and stay away as far as possible from negative people. If you are still around negative people when you know it is not the right thing to do, then it means you want their approval more than taking care of your mind.

When you take good care of yourself in all areas of your life, then you will feel good because there is nothing negative that will make you feel bad about yourself. For example, when you consume healthy foods, your body will feel good, which means you will feel good. When you are around positive people, they will make you feel good, which means you will feel good about yourself. The more you take care of yourself, the more you will feel good about yourself from the inside and out.

"The very best thing you can do for the whole world is to make the most of yourself."

Wallace D. Wattles

(Author of "The Science of Being Great")

If you have trouble taking good care of yourself, then try applying the following action steps:

ACTION STEPS

1. List down every aspect of your life (body, mind, spirit, emotion, etc.)

2. On each category, list everything down you would need to do to take good care of it

3. For each area, come up with at least two ways on how you can learn and make it better. You want to research not only on how to apply the knowledge, but also the benefits. You want to make sure you know the benefits of your actions to help keep your motivation up

4. Keep on learning, adding, and applying until you applied and mastered what you want to accomplish in all of your areas in order to take good care of yourself

Section 2: Your Belief System

Words of Commitments

Self-esteem is considered the ability to value and believe in yourself; this includes your beliefs and values. In order for your self-esteem to increase, you have to make sure your beliefs and values get stronger. The only way to do that is through taking action. Every time you take action that matches your own beliefs and values, the higher your self-esteem will become; even if a negative outcome is the result.

If you have trouble taking action that should match your own beliefs and values, then it means that you tend to break your commitments and promises to yourself and other people.

You have been influenced by society to believe that it is okay to lie, and that lying will not hurt anyone. However, the person who is going to get hurt the most when you lie is yourself. As a human being, you are unlikely to take action to keep your commitments when you lie because you do not believe in what you are saying. Even though the commitment is to another person, it is still your commitment because you made it, and not the other person. In this case, you are breaking yourself when you do not keep your commitments, which mean you are breaking your self-esteem.

Even the smallest lies and commitments matter. For example, if you say you will be at your friend house at 2pm, but do not arrive there until 3pm, then you have lied, and then your self-esteem level will decrease. Or if you say you will finish reading your book in one week, but did not finish until 3 weeks later, then your self-esteem level will decrease. The longer apart you accomplish something from your commitment, the lower your self-esteem level will become.

However, not only will you have a high level of self-esteem when you take action in what you say, you will be able to accomplish many things in life. Every time you take action to what you are saying, you are telling to the world and most importantly to yourself that you can accomplish anything that you say you will do.

It was discovered that to accomplish anything in life, it is not the lack of knowledge or skill, but it is the lack of keeping your commitments and taking action in what you are saying. Have you ever set goals to do this and that, but never seem to be able to accomplish them? If you say yes, then it is because you cannot seem to keep your commitments in your daily life. In order to accomplish something big, you have to master the little things first, which are the daily things that you say and set out to do. How are you going to be able to accomplish something big when you cannot accomplish something small? In this case, the more you keep your words of commitments, the higher your self-esteem level will be. With a high level of self-esteem, you can achieve anything.

If you have trouble keeping your words of commitments, then try applying the following action steps:

ACTION STEPS

1. Write down everything you said you are going to do for yourself and other people

2. Keep track on how many commitments you accomplished and failed

   o The ones that you failed, re-evaluate your commitments

   o Do you make commitments just to impress other people?

   o Do your commitments and actions match your beliefs and values?

When you see your failures on paper, you are more likely to want to change. As you start to keep your commitments to yourself and other people, you will feel amazing about yourself. The more amazing you feel about yourself, the higher your self-esteem will be.

Follow Your Belief System

"Follow your bliss and the universe wills open doors for you where there were only walls."

Joseph Campbell

(Author of "The Power of Myth")

As a human being, you like to be prepared. When you are not prepared, you tend to be afraid because you do not know where you are going. In this case, the future is what you are afraid of because it is the unknown. How can you prepare for something when you do not know what will happen?

With a lack of preparation, you tend to go in multiple directions or in circles, which will make you really tired and frustrated. For example, it is like when you are driving to a new location without directions or a GPS. You are more likely to be afraid because you do not know where you are going. And then, you are more likely to go in circles and end up quitting because it makes you really tired and frustrated.

However, you do not need to know what will happen in the future to be prepared. Actually, you are already prepared. You already have the answers to everything. And those answers should come from your belief system. A belief system is simply a collection of things and thoughts that you believe are true. When something happens, you just need to act accordingly to what you believe is true in the present moment.

"You are an ocean knowledge hidden in a dew drop."

Jalaluddin Rum

(Author of "The Essential Rumi")

When you follow your belief system and it turns out to be a negative experience, then it is important that you do not beat yourself up. If you had a negative experience, then it only means you applied a belief that did not support your life. In this case, you want to make sure your belief system is filled with positive beliefs for yourself to help prevent making negative decisions.

If you want to have a positive belief system, then try applying the following action steps:

ACTION STEPS

1. Write down every single thing that went wrong or you want more improvement on

2. For each one, come up with at least 2 ways on how you can educate yourself to find a better belief that will fit your life

Education will provide you will different methods to test out to see which is right and wrong so you can choose what to put into your belief system. You should never stop educating yourself because new information will always be forming that will improve your belief system. In this case, education should be an ongoing learning process. When you have a positive belief system, you will not only become less afraid of the future, but you will make the right decision for yourself.

3. Write down your new belief

Beliefs and Goals

In order to accomplish your goals, they depend on your actions that depend on your beliefs. In this case, you want to make sure your beliefs help you accomplish your goals. If you have beliefs that do not support your goals, then how are you going to take the right actions? For example, if you want to improve your math skill, then some of your beliefs should be to practice solving math problems or get a math tutor. However, if your belief is to read a science book to improve your math skill, then how can you ever improve it? In this case, you want to make sure your beliefs match your goals.

If you want to know if your beliefs match your goals or not, then try applying the following action steps:

ACTION STEPS

1. Discover what your goal is

Sometimes what you want to accomplish has more than one goal. For example, if your goal is weight loss to become a healthier person, then you have two goals; weight loss and becoming a healthier person. Weight loss and becoming a healthier person are two different goals. You can lose weight and not become a healthier person. So you have to decide which one you want to accomplish first. You want to make sure you only focus on one goal at a time.

2. Write down your beliefs that should match your goal

For example, if your goal is to become a healthier person, then what are your beliefs in becoming a healthier person? Some ways to become a healthier person are to develop a healthy diet, exercise, and reduce stress. However, if you apply unhealthy behaviors such as skipping meals or consuming unhealthy foods, then you are not becoming a healthier person. Those behaviors are just the opposite of what a healthy person is.

Whenever you have a positive goal, but apply negative behaviors, then you are contradicting yourself, which will prevents you from accomplishing your goal. You simply cannot get a positive result through negative behaviors.

Another goal example is when you want to become a better parent. Most people believe that hitting and yelling are appropriate discipline methods to help their children learn. However, most people know that hitting and yelling are not positive behaviors, no matter what the situation is. Even though your children might listen to you when you hit or yell at them, you are not becoming a better parent. The only way you can become a better parent is when you apply positive skills, not negative.

Before you take action to fulfill your goal, you have to make sure your beliefs match your goal. If you have a positive goal, then make sure your beliefs are positive.

When your goal and belief match, you will become successful.

The Power of Education

You probably have heard often that education is a powerful tool, which will help you become a smarter person, right? If that is the case, then how come so many people believe that going to school to get an education is a waste of their time? Did they learn enough? Or perhaps, did they learn the wrong things?

It is not what you learn that is wrong or not enough, it is because you did not see the knowledge improving your life.

In order for something to benefit you, you have to apply it into your life; otherwise your knowledge becomes useless. However, when you went to school to get an education, the school system failed to teach and show you how to apply the knowledge into your lifestyle. And that is why you believe that going to school is a waste of your time.

Education is just the beginning. Education just provides you the direction to do something, but the power comes from how much you apply it into your lifestyle. For example, it is like a GPS. The GPS gives you the directions to a destination, but you have to follow and apply the directions in order to get to your destination. Otherwise, the GPS is useless. In this case, education is useless if you do not apply it. However, the more you apply what you have learned, the more powerful you will become.

"Knowing is not enough, we must apply. Wishing is not enough, we must do."

Johann Von Goethe

(Author of "The Elective Affinities")

Also, it is important that you apply what you have learned because that is the best way to know if you understand something or not. For example, there are many things in life that you know you should do, but you are not applying them. The main reason for this is because you did not fully understand how to apply the information.

"We learn by doing."

Aristotle

(Author of "On the Soul")

If you having trouble applying knowledge that you believe will benefit you, then try applying the following action steps:

ACTION STEPS

1. Write down everything that you believe you should do that will improve your life

2. For each one that you are not applying into your lifestyle, make a list of the benefits on how that knowledge can improve your life

3. Come up with at least 2 ways on how you can learn more about the knowledge to increase your understanding

4. Come up with at least 2 ways on how you can apply the knowledge into your life

5. Keep on learning and applying until you applied and mastered the knowledge into your lifestyle

Learning and Fun

Do you think that learning is boring? Are you tired of learning or going to school? Do you believe that the main purpose of learning is to get a degree or certificate in order to get a better job?

If you believe that learning is a boring thing that does not bring you happiness, then you have been learning things that you are not interested in. Or you have been influenced to believe that the main purpose of learning is to get a degree or certificate.

If you ever wondered where the influences came from, it started when you were young. The moment you were able to understand and comprehend, your parents would rush you off to school to get a degree as soon as possible without giving you the opportunity to decide what interest you. As a young person with little knowledge and also want to get your parents approval, you end up listening to them and rushing off to get a degree without knowing what you want to learn. You just went with the career that most people are in. And then, you end up learning something that you dislike. As a result, learning becomes like a chore that prevents you to want to continue on learning.

However, the main purpose of learning is to help you grow and become a happier person. Happiness requires you to grow. When you stop on learning, you stop on growing; this means your happiness stops on growing.

If you think learning is boring, then try applying the following action steps to help you turn learning into a fun experience:

ACTION STEPS

1. List down every single thing that you are currently learning at the moment or want to learn

2. Go through each item individually, and think and see yourself in the next 5 or 10 years, and ask yourself if are you still interested in learning the same subject or not? If you don't see yourself learning and improving on the same subject in the next 5 or 10 years, then what you are learning is not enjoyable to you. When you are interested in something, you would always have the desire to improve for the long term or even for the rest of your life. As you keep on improving and growing on the same subject, that subject will also becomes stronger and stronger, which means your happiness also becomes stronger.

Section 3: Making Decisions

Make Your Own Decisions

"Indecision is the thief of opportunities."

Jim Rohn

(American entrepreneur, author and motivational speaker)

Have you ever encountered times when you know what you should do, but you still insisting on getting other people opinions? Have you ever regretted taking someone else advice because your advice was better than the other person?

If you end up choosing other people's advice over yours, it is not because your advice was bad, but you have been influenced by other people. There will be times when other people opinions will affect you without you realizing it. For example, when you wait too long to make a decision, you will soon be influenced to make decision based on other people opinions. The longer you wait to make a decision; the more influenced you will become.

Many times, the moment that somebody begins to hear what your problem is, they will give you their opinions, and then, the influence begins. After you have heard so many opinions, you will get confused because you will not know which opinion is right for you. The worst part is that you will start to believe that your decision comes from you, but it actually comes from other people. A good example is advertisements. When advertisements are already influencing you, your decision is based on what the advertisements are saying, and less from you.

When it comes to your life, if your decision is not coming from you, then you are more likely to make the wrong decision. No one understands what you are going through better than yourself. It does not matter how much you explain your situation to people, they will never understand the situation better than you.

There are two main reasons why other people will not understand your situations better than you. First, you will never be able to tell 100% of the story. When something is passed down to another person, it will never be the same. Second, it is your human fear to be vulnerable. When you share 100% about yourself or your problem, other people might not appreciate you because your negative side is exposed. As a result, you many tend to hold off on some information about yourself or problem. Sometimes, you may believe that you are 100% sharing about your problem, but there is a good chance that you are not. When you hold out information, other people will not be able to understand your situation well. As a result, they cannot advise you the best solution for your problem.

In this case, you have to make your own decision without other people influences. The only time when the decision is based solely on you is when you make the decision at the beginning when your brain has not been influenced yet. You have to trust yourself that you can solve your own problem because you already have all the solutions within you. In life, whenever you have a problem, you will also have the solution for it. You cannot have one without the other. For example, you have learned in the chapter on "Self-Acceptance," there are two sides to everything. If a problem develops, a solution will develop. In life, everything has to stay in balanced.

"Trust yourself. You know more than you think you do."

Benjamin Spock

(Author of "A Better World for Our Children")

"Trust your hunches. They're usually based on facts filed away just below the conscious level."

Joyce Brothers

(Author of "Positive Plus: The Practical Plan for Liking Yourself Better")

"Self-trust is the first secret of success."

Ralph Waldo Emerson

(Author of "Self-Reliance")

If you have trouble trusting yourself to find solutions for your problems, then try applying the following action steps:

ACTION STEPS

1. Whenever a problem develops, immediately write down all of the solutions that you came up with by yourself. Think to yourself what would be the best solution for you to help you solve the problem. You can also do your own research, but do not ask your family or friends, or any other person for advice.
2. After you gather all of your solutions, pick one.
3. Take action right away with the solution you had picked

If you need help with the solution that you have picked, then you can ask for help. However, you have to make sure you stick to your solution that you had picked. People are only there to help you with your solution, not to be influenced to pick a different solution. If no one agrees to help you with your solution, then you would rather try to accomplish it by yourself than changing

your solution. The only time you can change your
solution is after you have failed.

Be 100% Committed

"You need to make a commitment, and once you make it, then life will give you some answers."

Les Brown

(Author of "Live Your Dreams")

Have you ever gotten afraid that your decision may turn out wrong, and then, you did not take any action at all? Do you ever feel like the more you delay the more you start to question yourself that your decision might not be any good?

If you would like to be less afraid of your decisions, then there are two things that you should do.

First, you want to be 100% committed to your decision. The main reason why your brain develops fear is because you are confused on which direction to follow. The brain needs something to follow in order not to develop fear. Another reason why you might be afraid to be 100% committed to your decision is because you think that you may not have the skill and knowledge to become successful.

However, you already have all the skill and knowledge within you to become successful. In order for your brain to unleash the skill and knowledge, you have to be 100% committed to your decision. The more you are committed to your decision, the faster your brain will unleash the skill and knowledge for you.

"The world has the habit of making room for the man whose actions show that he knows where he is going."

Napoleon Hill

(Author of "Think and Grow Rich")

"Once you make a decision, the universe conspires to make it happen."

Ralph Waldo Emerson

(Author of "Society and Solitude")

Second, you should take immediate action. When you do not take action, the brain will also start to get confused and developed doubt if you will stick to your decision or not. It is important to take action right away at the beginning when your brain did not produce as much fear yet compared to when you put it off. The longer you procrastinate to take action, the more fear your brain will develop that will influence you to start questioning yourself. A fearful mind is a confused mind that will prevent you to take action. The sooner you take action, the lesser fear your brain will develop that will be easier for you to take action and move forward.

"Doubt can only be removed by action."

Johann Wolfgang von Goethe

(Author of "The Elective Affinities")

"Action is the foundation key to all success."

Pablo Picasso

(Famous Painter and Artist in the 20th Century)

To help you be 100% committed to your decisions, then try applying the following action steps:

ACTION STEPS

1. Write down your goal

2. Research and list down all of the options on how you can accomplish your goal

3. Choose the best option from the list and then write down all of the steps you would need to do to accomplish your goal

4. Take action right away

Do What Feel Right

"To fulfill your destiny, stay tune to your heart. Don't let anyone squeeze you into a mold."

Joel Osteen

(Author of "Become a Better You")

Have you ever encountered times when your brain was telling you no or giving you fear about doing what you feel is right?

When that happens, it means your heart and brain is not communicating correctly with each other. As a result, it will be difficult for you to decide on what you should do because your brain and heart is telling you to do different things. And then, you would ask other people for their opinions on what you should do. However, when you ask other people for their opinions to what is better for you, it means you are asking other people what will bring you happiness.

Happiness can only be felt within your heart. Since no one knows how your heart feels, then they will not know what will bring you happiness, but only yourself. In this case, all you need to do is to listen to your heart and what it is telling you to do. Your heart is pure that cannot be influenced, which means you will always make the right decision for yourself if you follow your heart.

"When you follow the dream in your heart, you're energized, inspired, and motivated."

John F. Demartini

(Author of "The Breakthrough Experience")

There are two main reasons why your brain might think differently than your heart. Firstly, it has been influenced by other people. When people keep on giving you the same advice over and over again, your brain will start to believe that other people advice is true. As a result, your brain will tell you to follow other people opinions. A good example would be advertisements. If you are exposure to the same advertisements over and over again, soon or later you will start to believe what the advertisements are saying. Another example would be if you are around smokers. When you are constantly around smokers, your brain will start to think that smoking is okay. Sooner or later, you will become a smoker yourself; even though your heart is telling you not to.

The second reason why your brain might think differently than your heart is because of your human need to be accepted and belonged among other people. If you do not fulfill this human need, you will encounter suffering. In this case, there will be times when your brain will tell you to do things just to impress other people in order to be accepted.

If you have trouble following your heart, then try applying the following action steps:

ACTION STEPS

1. Write down all of your goals

2. Look at each goal individually, and ask yourself these questions:

   a. Does it make you suffer when you are not able to accomplish your goal? If you do not feel the suffering from not accomplishing your goal, then it is not from your heart.

   b. Do you feel like it is not a big deal if you do not accomplish your goal? If it is not a big deal, then it is not from your heart.

   c. Do you think about your goal often, at least 2 or 3 times per day? You should be thinking about your goal at least 2 or 3 times per day.

   d. Do you think how wonderful it would be if you are able to accomplish your goal? You should be thinking how yours and other people lives would be better off if you are able to accomplish your goal.

e. Are you afraid to fail to achieve your goal? When you are afraid, it means you will become a happier person at the end of the road when you accomplish your goal. Fear is a sign that it is out of your comfort zone.

The Right Decision for You

Sometimes making the right decision can be difficult when you are caught in between making other people or yourself happy because you cannot do both at once. When you decide to do things for yourself, you develop a selfishness feeling from within that creates a lot of suffering for you. On the other hand, when you do things for other people, you also suffer because you are not doing things that make you happy. As a result, it does not matter what you decide to do, you end up suffering. The main reason for this conflict is because of your human need to be accepted by other people.

If you have ever been faced between making other people or yourself happy, then you should try to understand that you and other people are one, which is known as "Inter-being." Inter-being means that everyone and everything is connected with each other. "Inter" means connect, and "Being" means human beings or living things. This term comes from the teaching of Zen Master Thich Nhat Hanh on Engaged Buddhism. It does not matter what you decide to do, you and the other party will experience the same kind of feelings at the end. When you do something, either negative or positive, it affects everyone and everything around you. If you are happy, other people will also become happy. If you are sad, other people will also become sad. Other people happiness and sadness are also your happiness and sadness. For example, if you pay attention, when one of your family members is going through a stressful time, everyone in the family will be stressed out. The reason for this is because you and your family are connect. And happiness is the same thing. When you experience happiness, everyone will also experience happiness.

"We are not independent but inter-dependent."

Thich Nhat Hanh

(Author of "Peace is Every Step")

To help you make the right decisions for yourself, try applying the following action steps.

ACTION STEPS

1. Write down all of your goals

2. Write down action steps that only move you toward your goals

If you are taking actions that are not getting you closer to your goals, then basically you are making decisions to impress other people. When you a make decision to take action, stay focus and trust your intuition in the present moment.

Whatever you decide to do something in your life, if you believe in your heart that you are making the right decision in the present moment, then you should not feel guilty for any reason; even if a negative outcome is the result. Whenever you feel uncomfortable making decisions that come from your heart, it is only because of your human need to be accepted. However, your uncomfortable feelings are just like any other feeling, it will come, but it will also go away.

If you follow your heart, you are most likely will make the right decision. Sometimes the decision could be for you, while other times they could be for other people. Also, be patient with yourself and other people because sometimes the benefits do not manifest right away.

Be in Control

"Put your future in good hand --- your own"

Mark Victor Hansen

(Co-Author of "Chicken Soup for the Soul")

What does it mean when you are in control of your life? Does it mean that you always have to make the right decision? Does it mean there is no set back in your life? Does it mean you do not allow things to get worst?

Even though you might want things to always turn out correctly or there is no setback in your life, being in control of your life does not mean things have to go as planned or you have to make the right decision all the time.

Being in control means accepting what is in the present moment, positive or negative, and move forward from there. You have probably encountered many times in your life that things do not always go as planned, but that does not mean you are not in control of the situation or your life. For example, when you decide to host a party and you have 100 reservations. However, only 50 people show up. As a result, things did not turn out as planned. Even though you might feel a little bit disappointed that only half show up, you still continue with the party and rearrange certain things to fit the party better with only 50 people. In this case, you are still in control of the party.

If you want to be in control of your life, then there are two things you should do. First, you have to make your own decision. Second, you have to take 100% responsibility for your decisions and actions.

You have to make your own decisions in your life. If you allow people to make your decisions for you, then it means other people are controlling your life, not you. Also, when you do not make your own decisions, then it means that you are afraid that you will not have the ability and strength to handle whatever the outcome is.

Whatever the result is, whether it is positive or negative; you have to take 100% responsibility for your actions. If you are not taking responsibility for your actions, then that also means you believe you do not have the ability and strength to tackle and solve your own problems. Taking responsibility does not mean that you have to know all the answers right away, but that you are willing to find the answers to solve your problems and not let them hold you back from moving forward in life. Sometimes it might take you awhile to fix something, but as long as you are fixing your problems and moving forward every day, then you are in control of your life.

"Happy people are those who feel truly terrific about themselves and this is the natural outgrowth of accepting responsibility for their life."

Brian Tracy

(Author of "The Ultimate Success Guide")

If you have trouble being in control of your life, then try applying the following action steps:

ACTION STEPS

1. Write down all of your problems that you need and want to be in control of

2. For each problem, lists down all the options to solve it

3. Pick one option and then take action right away to be in control of your problem

4. If the first one does not work, keep on trying something else until you find the right solution for your problem

Section 4: Making Mistakes

True Meaning of a Negative Experience

"There is no failure – just experience and your reactions to them."

Thomas Krause

(Author of "Touching Hearts-Teaching Greatness, "A Teen's Guide to NOT Being Perfect")

Are you afraid to take actions because you might have a negative experience that could make your life worse? Are you afraid to take risks because there is a chance that you could fail? Do you believe your negative experience will turn you into a negative person?

If you ever stop yourself from taking action just because your situation might result in a negative outcome, then you have been influenced by society to believe that negative experiences are bad. Society has put a bad repetition on negative experiences because the word negative is categorized as a bad term. As a result, you are unlikely to take action unless you know that there will be a positive outcome at the end. You are afraid that when you have a negative experience, you would then become a negative or bad person.

A negative or bad person is when you know something is wrong and still take action anyway. However, when you decide to take action and believe it is the right thing to do, then you are not a bad person, and it does not matter if a negative outcome is the result.

Even though you would rather have a positive outcome, it does not matter what happen, positive or negative, they are just terms that you label for yourself. If you choose to label everything positive, then everything in your life will become positive. If you choose to label everything negative, then everything in your life will become negative. It is all up to you on how you label your experiences.

If you ever find yourself having a difficult time taking actions because of your fear of having a negative outcome, then try applying the following action steps:

ACTION STEPS

1. Write down your goal

2. Come up with 2 positive outcomes if you were to take action to achieve your goal

3. Come up with 3 different ways on how to help you get started to accomplish your goal

4. Write down the negative outcome if you were to take action to achieve your goal

5. Come up with 3 different ways on how to prevent the negative outcome to happen

6. Take action right away to make sure you achieve your goal with the positive outcome as the result

Mistakes and Opportunities

"In every negative event is the seed of an equal of greater benefit."

Napoleon Hill

(Author of "The Law of Success")

"Inside of every problem lies an opportunity."

Robert Kiyosaki

(Author of "Rich Dad Poor Dad")

Do you ever feel like you have to make the right decision all the time? If not, are you afraid that other people will not appreciate and accept you? Do you unconsciously make yourself feel bad when you make mistakes because you think you did something terrible and that you deserve to feel the pain?

As a human being, you have to understand that you will make mistakes no matter how well you prepare yourself because you are not perfect. Also, you have to remember that mistakes are not negative things, but experiences from a misunderstanding to tell you not to repeat the same things over again. If you can change and improve from your mistakes, then you should not feel guilty about making them. For example, it is like when a child makes the mistake of touching a hot stove for the very first time. After his mistake, he understood that he should not touch the hot stove again. As long as he learned from his mistake and not repeats it over again, then he has nothing to be ashamed of or feel guilty about. It is only when the child touches the hot stove again after his mistake, then he should feel guilty.

It is very important that you forgive yourself for the mistakes after you have learned from them. When you punish yourself, it is more difficult for you to move forward in life. In addition, the great advantage of making mistakes is that it will give you the opportunities to learn and grow, which means your happiness will also grow. Every time you overcome something, your knowledge, courage, and creativity levels will increase.

"You gain strength, courage and confidence by every experience in which you really stop to look fear in the face."

Eleanor Roosevelt

(Longer Former First Lady of the United States from 1933-1945)

To help you overcome your mistakes and grow, try applying the following action steps:

ACTION STEPS

1. Write down your mistakes
2. Write down what you would do differently the next time you encounter the same situation

By writing it down, your brain will be able to see clearly on what you will do differently the next time the same situation happens again, so you can avoid making the same mistake. When you encounter the same problem, the brain does not have to waste time coming up with a better solution because you already have it written down. In this case, you will have more time and energy to fix your problem. If not, when the same problem happens again, your brain will be too busy worrying about the problem to come up with a better solution.

Being Good with a Bad Repetition

Have you ever encountered times when people put you down for doing the right things? Have you ever feel embarrassed for doing the right things? Have you ever done negative things on purpose to try to fit in with other people?

When people put you down for doing the right things, there are three main reasons why. First, people cannot do the same positive things themselves. When you are better than other people, they will feel uncomfortable. In order for people to get out of the uncomfortable zone, it is easier for them to put you down than to compliment you. Negative talks are faster at numbing negative emotions compared to positive encouragements. For example, when you are stressing out, negative behaviors such as smoking or consuming sweet or fatty foods will numb your emotions quicker than engaging into positive behaviors such as going for a walk or other positive activities. When other people make excuses why they do negative things, it is only to numb their unpleasant feelings to make them feel better about themselves because they cannot do the right things.

Second, they are not happy people. When you are a happy person, you will acknowledge other people for their positive behaviors, not put them down. In addition, you will use that knowledge to help you understand yourself and other people better.

Third, they believe that you are trying to be perfect. As human beings, it is normal for everyone to make mistakes; so people would believe that by doing negative things is the same thing as making mistakes. As a result, when people behave negatively, they believe that their behaviors are mistakes that make it okay for them to do so.

However, making mistakes and engaging in negative behaviors are two very different things. Mistakes occur when you believe your action is right from the beginning, but then it turns out to be wrong. For example, if you want to experiment something that you have never done before that turns out negative, then that is a mistake. For example, if you are a child touching a hot stove for the very first time and not knowing that it is hot, then that is a mistake. However, if you touch the hot stove again, then that is a negative behavior. When you know that your action will result in a negative outcome at the beginning, but you still insisting on taking action anyway, then that is a negative behavior, not a mistake, and it does not matter what kind of excuses you make.

When you do the right things, it does not mean you are trying to be perfect because you know you are not. If you are were able to always do positive things, then your life will be perfect, but it is not. In addition, when you purposely try to do negative things, then you are harming yourself because you are doing things that you do not believe in.

Even though other people might accept you at the beginning when you behave negatively; they will not enjoy you for the long term. Positive behaviors might take a longer time to benefit you, but when the benefits manifest, other people will want to be around you for a longer periods of time.

"It is not true that nice guys finish last. Nice guys are winners before the game even starts."

Addison Walker

(Creator of the comic strips the "Bettle Bailey" in 1950)

If you feel bad when other people put you down for doing the right things, then try applying the following action steps:

ACTION STEPS

1. Write down all of your negative behaviors that you do to try to fit in or impress other people

2. For each negative behavior, write down all the negative outcomes that could happen in your life

3. Write down the positive behaviors that other people are putting you down when you do them

4. For each positive behavior, write down the positive outcomes that could happen in your life

5. Write down all the people who give you negative comments when you do the right things. And then try to stay away from those people as much as possible

6. Stay focus on the positive outcomes from your positive behaviors

Knowing When to Change YOU

"The moment you start changing to please people, you will be taking a step backward."

Joel Osteen

(Author of "Your Best Life Now")

Have you ever heard a negative comment about yourself, and then you ran off to try to change yourself? If that happens, it is because you were raised in a family that is more focused on negative reactions than the positive. As a young child, whenever you do something positive, your parents are unlikely to celebrate for your success. They think that positive outcomes are normal that should not get much attention.

However, every time you do something wrong, your parents would put a lot of pressure on you to try to change you. If you do not change, you will get punished. At a young age, you will make a lot of mistakes, which means you will be pressured to change a lot. As a result, you build the habit to believe that you need to change every time someone gives you a bad comment.

When you reach adulthood and able to think for yourself, you will develop a conflict within yourself because of the habit. For example, when someone tells you to change, but as an adult, you believe that you should not change. However, when you do not change, you will feel guilty or ashamed because of the habit you developed to believe that you should change every time someone gives you a bad comment.

Did you know that when someone tells you to change, it is not you, but it is the other person who needs to change? The only reason why someone tells you to change is because they cannot control their negative emotions when you said or did something that they did not like. Whenever people feel uncomfortable, they want to change the situation instantly to get out of the uncomfortable zone. People would rather tell you to change instead of them, because it is easier for them. So, it is not for your own benefit when people tell you to change, but it is for their own benefits.

According to Dr. Daniel Amen who developed a simple rule called "18/40/60." He stated that "When you're 18, you worry about what everybody is thinking of you; when you're 40, you don't give a darn what anybody thinks of you; when you're 60, you realize nobody's been thinking about you at all."

If you really think about it, why would other people worry about your life when they have their own life to worry about? Taking care of one's self is more than enough work and responsibility already to have time to think about other people. In addition, if you are always worrying about what other people think of you, then you would not have enough time to worry about yourself.

Going back to the first chapter on "Self-Acceptance," when people tell you to change because of your negative qualities, it does not necessary mean those qualities are bad. It just simply means that other people already labeled something else positive, so these traits have to be labeled negative.

If you ever find yourself wanting to change because someone else tells you to change, then it means that you cannot control your negative emotions. When you hear negative comments about yourself, you will develop negative reactions that will make you feel uncomfortable that will influence you to want to change. However, it is important for you to learn how to embrace and accept your negative emotions because they are also a part of you. When you are able to embrace your negative emotions, it does not matter what other people are saying or doing, you will never feel uncomfortable, which means that you will never feel that you need to change.

Deep down in your heart, if you believe that you need to change, then you would change already without waiting for anyone to tell you to. When it is the right time for you to change, your heart will tell you.

"I will change when I wish or need to change, when the moment for change is ripe. Until then I will remain as I am."

Stacey Charter

(Motivational quotes writer and cancer survivor)

To help you from changing yourself when it is not the right time, try applying the following action step:

ACTION STEPS

1. Write down what people are saying that is negative about you, and then figure out how you can turn it into a positive quality

Let's take a closer look at a talkative person. If someone told you that being a talkative person is a negative thing, then think of situations where being talkative is a positive thing. For example, being talkative means that you are more comfortable being around other people and not afraid to share your opinions compared to another person who is shy. Sometimes, your high energy level will help ease up the environment to help other people who are shy to feel more comfortable to speak up and share.

When someone labels your qualities as negative, just rethink and see how those qualities can become positive. Remember, it does not matter what people say, there is always a positive side to everything. When you turn your negative qualities into positive, you will never have to change yourself ever again because what other people see as negative, they are positive to you.

Reward Yourself

Take a moment and think to yourself when you accomplished something when you were young or even as an adult; such as learning how to ride a bike or tie your shoe, or getting your first job; did your parents take the time to celebrate for your success?

Do you sometimes have trouble moving forward in life because you have done so many things for other people, but do not get the appreciation or acknowledgment that you think you deserve?

If you answer yes, then there are two main reasons why. First, as human beings, sometimes we would think that acknowledgement is not needed when we do the right things.

We think that doing positive things are expected and normal. For example, it is like eating. Eating is a way of living. When you eat, you do not get acknowledged for your eating behaviors; even though you might work hard to develop a healthy diet.

Second, other people might not see your accomplishments as worthy enough to be celebrated. As human beings, everyone has a different standard. If other people have higher standards than you, then they are unlikely to appreciate or acknowledge you for your success, despite how much you think you deserve the appreciation or acknowledgement.

However, as a human being, sometimes you would need acknowledgements for your successes in order to move forward. Since you cannot always count on other people, you need to acknowledge yourself for your successes.

Every success, small and big, should be acknowledged. Success does not mean you have to achieve something big. Success simply means you had accomplished something that you have never done before.

Acknowledgments will reinforce that you are a great human being with a lot of potential to become successful at great things. Even though you might feel better to be acknowledged and appreciated by other people for your success, you are the main person who should acknowledge and appreciate yourself. Other people's acknowledgement should only be extra and not be considered the most important.

One successful method of acknowledgement is to reward yourself. The reward could be anything; physical, mental, or spiritual, or any other way to keep your motivation up. However, there is a wrong and a right way to reward yourself. Make sure you reward yourself accordingly to your success that will help you move forward in life. For example, when you accomplish something small, then you should reward yourself something small. When you have a big accomplishment, then you should reward yourself something big. If you reward yourself in the wrong way, it could prevent you to move forward in life.

One way to know if you deserve the reward or not is by looking at the after effect of the reward. Everything you do in your life must have a purpose. For example, after you earned your degree, the reward could be a vacation. However, if your vacation does not motivate you to take your knowledge to do better things such as contributing to your community and society, then you did not deserve the vacation. The purpose of your vacation is to help recharge your energy and strength to prepare yourself so you can use your knowledge to contribute to your community and society. Rewarding is just a tool to keep your motivation up, it is not to set an end to your journey.

If you have trouble rewarding yourself for your success in order to move forward in life, then try applying the following action steps:

ACTION STEPS

1. List down all of your successes, small and big

2. List down everything that you would like to reward yourself with. It could be material, mental, or spiritual things that you would like to have or experience

3. If you have never reward yourself before, then look at your successes and choose one. Then look at your reward list, and then choose one that matches your success

4. As you accomplish new things, make sure to reward yourself accordingly to your reward list. Keep on adding new things to your reward list

Section 5: Creating a Positive Social Group

How to Attract Positive People

When someone dislikes you, it is because they are focusing more on your negative qualities than your positive qualities. If you are surrounded with more negative people, then it means that your negative qualities are stronger than your positive qualities.

As a human being, you tend to attract who you have become. It begins with how you feel about yourself. For example, if you feel negative, your negative qualities will become stronger that will turn you into a sad and depress person. And then, you will attract sad and depress people. On the other hand, if you feel positive, your positive qualities will manifest that will help you become a positive and happy person. And then, you will attract positive and happy people. So in this case, you want to make sure your positive qualities are develop and stronger than your negative qualities so you can attract only positive and happy people.

To help you develop and make your positive qualities stronger, try applying the following action steps:

ACTION STEPS

1. You want to make sure your positive qualities are developed. The best way to develop your positive qualities is for you to be yourself. When you are being yourself, you will develop a true sense of happiness that can only develop from within you that will make it easier for your positive qualities to unleash. The more you are being yourself, the happier you will become, the more your positive qualities will unleash. To help you to be yourself, try applying the following techniques:

    -   Stop worrying about what other people think about you

- Be clear about what make you happy

- Do only things that you will increase your happiness

- Act on what you know is right for yourself

- Never apologize for being you

"Be yourself, everyone else is already taken."

Oscar Wilde

(Author of "The Happy Prince and Other Tales")

2. Make sure your positive qualities are stronger than your negative qualities. In life, everything either grows or dies. If you do not make your positive qualities stronger, sooner or later they will become weak and fade away. To help you make your positive qualities stronger, try applying the following action steps:

a. Write down all of your positive qualities. Your positive qualities are anything that you consider positive to you; even though other people might think they are negative. They could also be your successes, small and big, because they tend to happen because of your positive qualities.

b. Review your list of positive qualities at least twice per day. The more the better. The more the brain sees your positive qualities, the more it will stay focus on them. Try to reinforce your positive qualities the first and last thing of the day to help build the habit. You want to start and end the day with a positive mindset.

c. Every time one or more of your negative qualities take your focus, just become aware that they are a part of you and then refocus back to your positive qualities.

Qualities of a True Friend

"Be careful the friends you choose for you will become like them."

W. Clement Stone

(Author of "Success through a Positive Mental Attitude")

Are there people in your life who you cannot decide if you should continue being friend with them or not? Do you sometimes end up with negative friends; even though your intention is to only have positive friends?

As a human being, you would rather have positive people in your life because you know that negative people can have a negative influence on you. You probably have heard the saying, "You become who you are surrounded with." If you are surrounded with negative people, soon you will become a negative person, and it does not matter how positive of a person you started out with. However, if you are surrounded with positive people, soon you will become a positive person, and it does not matter how negative of a person you started out with.

If you have trouble distinguish between negative and positive people, then go through the following check list:

QUALITIES OF A TRUE FRIEND

1. A true friend will always appreciate you no matter what happen, with no expectation in return.

2. A true friend does not try to change you because of your negative qualities. They can you give you their opinions, but nothing more.

3. A true friend will encourage you to do things that you are passionate about or help you solve problems that might be difficult.

4. A true friend will still want to be around you after disagreements because he or she sees that disagreements are opportunities to understand each other.

5. A true friend understands that you have the right to feel differently. It does not matter how similar you and your friend are, you and your friend are still two different people who will always have different opinions or viewpoints.

6. A true friend will allow you to feel comfortable to say "no" when something or someone make you feel uncomfortable.

"Having one good friend is worth more than being popular amongst many."

Carolynn Warner

(Founder and President of Corporate Education Consulting Inc.)

"It is better to be alone than in bad company."

George Washington

(The 1ˢᵗ President of the United States)

Show Other People How to Treat You

You would rather have other people treat you well than bad, right? Of course you would. However, how do people know how to treat you the way you want to be treated? Is it through what you tell people? It is through your behaviors and actions?

You probably have heard and learned that if you want other people to treat you well, then you have to treat other people well, the way that you would want to be treated. However, if that was the case, then why are there people who treated other people poorly? Do they want to be treated poorly?

Have you ever encountered times when you treat other people well, but do not get it back in return, and then, you stop treating other people well.

When people do not treat you well, it does not mean you are treating them poorly. As a human being, each of us has a different level of expectation in what it means to be treated well. When you believe that the way you treat other people is great, but do not get it back in return, then it means that the other person has a higher level of expectation of what treating well is. As a result, they are unlikely to treat you well in return because you did not meet their expectation.

If you want people to treat you accordingly to your standard, then the best way to show them is through how well you treat yourself. One of the best ways for people to learn and apply something is through seeing some kind of examples. When you treat yourself well, people will see exactly how you would like to be treated, and then they can do the same thing for you.

For example, if you are being kind to yourself, people will treat you kindly. If you are a calm person, people will also become calm when they are around you. If you are a positive person, people will treat you in a positive way. However, if you are always angry at yourself, people are more likely to become angry at you. Or, if you are a serious person, other people will become serious when they are around you.

"You train people how to treat you by how you treat yourself."

Martin Rutte

(President of the company Livelihood)

Another good example would be the way you eat. People are more likely to offer you foods that they often see you eat. People are unlikely to offer you something that they had never seen you eat before because they are afraid that you might not like it. So, if people see you eat hamburgers all the time, they will offer you hamburgers. However, if you are a healthy eater who always eats fruits and vegetables, then people will most likely offer you fruits and vegetables.

Or, if you are a messy person, people are less likely to clean their home when you visit them. They believe that their mess is not a big deal to you because that is how you are. However, if you are a neat person, people will try to make their homes as neat as possible for you when you visit them. If other people want you to come into their homes and you are a neat person, they will try to meet your expectation. As a result, when you are treating yourself well, everyone and everything around you will treat you according to your standard.

"The way you treat yourself sets the standard for others."

Sonya Friedman

(Author of "On a Clear Day You Can See Yourself: Turning the Life You Have into the Life You Want")

If people are not treating you well, then you should re-evaluate how you treat yourself. Do not be surprised if you have been treating yourself negatively. Sometimes you would treat yourself negatively without realizing it. To help you see if you are treating yourself well or not, then try applying the following action steps:

ACTION STEPS

1. Write down on how you would want other people to treat you

2. Go through each item individually to see if you are treating yourself the way you would want other people to treat you. For example, if you want other people not to get angry and forgive you when you make a mistake, then reflect back if you forgive yourself or not for your mistake. Or if you want other people to be positive around you, then ask yourself, are you a positive person yourself?

Fit In Or Not To Fit In

Do you ever feel like you are not a normal person when you look around and everyone has or doing the same thing, but not you? Do you start to question yourself that you should do what everyone else is doing in order to fit in and be accepted? Do you believe that being different from everyone else is not a good thing?

If you ever find yourself believing that you should be doing what everyone else is doing in order to bring you happiness, then you have been influenced. You believe that you need to fit in with everyone else; otherwise they would not want to be around you because you are different.

However, if you pay closely attention, most of the things that majority of people are doing or having, it is because of their habits that they cannot quit. As a human being, it is easy for you to build habits, but difficult to break them. And that is why you tend to have negative habits that you cannot seem to break. Habits can develop just by trying something once. At the beginning, you might believe that trying something once is not a big deal because you also believe that you will have the strength to quit if that thing does not bring you happiness. However, the moment you try something new, the habit begins.

Do not consider trying something new that you already have doubt that it will not bring you happiness, and it does not matter how many people are doing or having it. If something is good for you or will bring you happiness, you would get or start it at the beginning, and do not have to wait until for everyone else to do or have it in order for you to believe that it is a good thing for you.

Also, you have to remember that everyone is different, which means you would need different things in your life to bring you happiness. If everyone has or does the same thing, then everyone would be the same, but we are not. So whenever someone gives you bad comments on why you are not doing what everyone else is doing, then just remember that they are not mentally strong enough to avoid it or cannot break their habit.

In this case, you are a stronger person when you are not doing what everyone else is doing because you are not influenced by society. If you ever have doubt if something will bring you happiness or not, it is likely that whatever that thing is, it will not bring you happiness. When you encounter something new, your heart will know immediately if it will bring you happiness or not.

You have to be very caution with new things or people who will enter into your life because they can bring you a lot of suffering. The moment something enters into your life, it is difficult to get rid of it. Your life is precious, so do not let anything or anyone interrupt it.

To help you not to be influenced by everyone else, try applying the following action steps:

ACTION STEPS

1. Write down everything that everyone is doing, but not you

2. Write down all the negative things that could happen if you are doing what everyone else is doing

3. Write down all the positive things and people who are already in your life and stay focus on them.

"People laugh at me because I am different, I laugh at them because they are all the same."

Swami Vivekananad

(Author of "Inspired talks")

Everyone is Equally Powerful

"Just as much as we see in others we have in ourselves."

William Hazlitt

(Author of "Characters of Shakespeare")

Do you believe that some people are born to become natural leaders? Do you believe that you will never be as great as other people are? Do you believe that natural and powerful leaders deserve more acknowledgement and attention than you because you are not as great as them?

As human beings, everyone is born equally with one another – we are all born with the same level of greatness and the ability to become powerful leaders. The only difference is the strength and talent that each person is born with. For example, a math and a science teacher will teach different things, but they can become great at the same level. A mental and spiritual health practitioner can become great by teaching different things in their field of expertise.

"All of us do not have equal talent, but all of us should have an equal opportunity to develop our talents."

John F. Kennedy

(The 35th President of the United States)

It is not the lack of knowledge or strength that you are missing to become great, but it is how much you use and grow your own strength and talent in your life. If you pay attention, the thing that separates powerful leaders and everyone else is their ability to use their own strength and talent to the fullest to help themselves and other people constantly. Their life becomes a message to themselves and the world.

"My life is my message."

Mahatma Ghandi

(Preeminent leader and freedom fighter)

"What I want for myself, I want for everybody."

Wallace Wattles

(Author of "The Science of Being Great")

The more you apply your strength and talent, the stronger they will become, the more powerful you will become. For example, your strength and talent are like seeds. In order for the seeds to grow, you have to water them. In order for your strength and talent seeds to grow, you have to use them. When you keep on using your strength and talent, they will become stronger and stronger, and then, you will start to believe that you are as powerful as anyone else.

In this case, if everyone was to use their own strength and talent, then no one is more successful or talented than anyone else because everyone contributes equally to society by using different strength and talent.

There are two advantages when you believe you are powerful through using your own strength and talent. First, you will have an opened mind to learn and improve yourself from everyone and everything. You approach other people as equal with the opportunity to learn from them because they have different strength and talent that you do not have.

Second, you will have the ability to distinguish and block out information that might not benefit you. However, if you believe that you are not as great as other people, you are more likely to be influenced by them because you believe that your life should be the same as them because their life is so great.

If you do not see yourself as equal and powerful as other people, then try applying the following action steps:

ACTION STEPS

1. Write down all of your strength and talent, small and big

2. Research and write down at least two ways on how you can apply your strength and talent into your life

3. Research and write down at least two ways on how you can apply your strength and talent to help other people

4. Write down how would yours and other people life would be different in a negative way if you are not able to apply and share your strength and talent

5. Write down how would yours and other people life would be different in a positive way if you are able to apply and share your strength and talent

6. After you accomplished and mastered the two ways to your life and to help other people, keep on adding new ways on how you can apply and share your strength and talent to help yourself and other people

Section 6: True Happiness

True Happiness

"There is only one person who could ever make you happy, and that person is you."

David Burns

(Author of "The Feeling Good: The New Mood Therapy")

"Nothing can bring you happiness but yourself."

Ralph Waldo Emerson

(Author of "Self-Reliance")

Have you ever lost someone who you love or admire, and then you believe that in order to get that happiness back, you have to find someone else to replace that person? Or have you ever think to yourself that if you lost or cannot have this or that, then you would not be happy?

If you ever found yourself believing that you have to find someone or to get this or that in order to bring you happiness, then you are counting on external factors to bring you happiness.

However, happiness can only exist within you. You are the only person who can bring yourself happiness. Even though other people or things might make or bring you some pleasure, they are not happiness.

"It is not easy to find happiness in ourselves, and it is not possible to find it elsewhere."

Agnes Repplier

(Author of "Books and Men")

"What lies behind us and what lies before us are tiny matters compared to what lies within us."

Ralph Waldo Emerson

(Author of "Society and Solitude"

When you rely on other people for your happiness, you are taking the risk on your own happiness. Your happiness could be gone in any second because other people could decide to walk out of your life at any time because you do not have control over them. However, the happiness that you can always control and have forever is the happiness that you develop within yourself. No one can take away your happiness when you are the one creating it.

"No one outside ourselves can rule us inwardly. When we know this, we become free."

Thich Nhat Hanh

(Author of "Peace is every step")

According to the happiness theory, 75% of happiness is based on your strength, courage, and confidence, and how well you treat yourself. The last 25% is from external factors such as materialism and other people.

So when you develop, build, and keep your happiness within yourself, then it does not matter what happen or how other people treat you, no one and nothing can take your happiness away. In addition, when you have happiness within you, you will have the strength and courage to move forward in life quicker when someone makes you suffer compared when you do not have happiness within you.

"When there is no enemy within, the enemies outside cannot hurt you."

African Proverb

To help build your happiness, try applying the following action steps:

ACTION STEPS

1. Write down what you want to accomplish that you are afraid to fail. These include taking risks, challenges, or things that require you to be out of your comfort zone

2. For each one, research and develop an action plan for it

3. Write down how would your life be different in a positive way if you are able to accomplish what you are afraid of

4. Take action right away

This is your chance to do things that you think you cannot do. As a human being, you may tend to underestimate your ability. In this case, whatever you think you cannot do, you can do it. The only reason why you think you cannot do something is because of your fear of the unknown. When you take action in spite of fear, the strength and courage at the end will be so amazing. Even though the results might not be as what you wanted, that does not matter as much because strength and courage increase every time you take fearful action. You do not need to accomplish your goals to increase your strength and courage.

"If people believe in themselves, it's amazing what they can accomplish."

Sam Walton

(Founder of Wal-Mart and Sam's Club)

Gratification vs. Happiness

Do you think that it is important for you to take action in order to improve your community or society? Have you ever stop yourself from taking action to try to improve your community or society because you believe that one person cannot make a difference? Do you feel like it would be a waste of your time to take action by yourself?

If you have ever stop yourself from taking action to improve your community or society because you believe that you as one person cannot make a difference, then you are seeking for gratification, not happiness. You believe that there must be a significant result or outcome at the end in order for you to take action.

However, as a human being, your main goal is to seek for happiness, not gratification. Happiness depends on how strong your feelings and beliefs are toward your actions, and not on the result or outcome.

You might already know that external thing such as materialism will not bring you happiness. In this case, results or outcomes are also considered external things that can only give you gratification, not happiness.

If you are one person taking action, and you believe in your actions that will improve your community and society, then that will bring you happiness. You do not need to wait to see the result to manifest in order to experience happiness. Outside results or outcomes can be used as a motivation to help you take action and move forward only.

The true benefit that you should seek and receive is the feelings that you develop from your actions. When you believe in what you are doing is the right thing, then your happiness should develop the moment you take action. If you do not receive the happiness right away when you take action, it means you are counting on results or outcomes to bring you happiness, which means you are seeking for gratification.

Also, if you believe that one person cannot make a difference, then you are wrong. If you are contributing to your community and society, the result will manifest, but it might not be visible for you to see. Sometimes your actions affect other people or parts of the community that you do not see or aware of. When you take positive actions, they will lead to positive results.

If you have trouble taking actions, then try applying the following action steps:

ACTION STEPS

1. List down on how you would want your community and society to be

2. Write down what would it takes to accomplish what you want

3. Look at your list and start taking action right away, do your part

For example, if you want your community and society to have a cleaner environment, then do your part by not littering. Or if you know that it is better to walk or bike to nearby locations to reduce air pollution than driving, then do your part to walk or bike. Or if you know that it is important for everyone to vote, then do your part to vote. It is all about doing your part. If everyone was to do their part, then imagine how your community and society will change massively. Remember that everything beings will one person.

"What you get by achieving your goals is not as important as what you become by achieving your goals."

Zig Ziglar

(Author of "Better Than Good: Creating a Life You Can't Wait to Live")

Outside Images

In life, words and things mean differently to each person. The meanings all depend on you. For example, when you say the word "flower," each person will think and have a different image. One person would think that the flower will smell good. Another person would think that the flower is a pretty thing. Or another person would think that it is for decoration. In this case, the flower has many meanings. Whatever your meaning is for the flower, it is up to you.

Whatever you want to achieve for yourself, it depends on your own definition. For example, if you want to become successful, it depends on your definition of success. When you use other people definition of success, it will be difficult for you to achieve it because you are trying to achieve someone else success. Even though other people definition of success is not bad, it is still not yours definition. It is the same with happiness; each person will have a different idea what will bring them happiness.

You have to give up the outside images in order to figure out what you consider success or happiness is. You want to stay focused on your own definition. Even though society has standards for what success and happiness are, you do not have to follow those standards if you do not believe in them. It does not matter how many people have the same standards on success and happiness, if they do not fit in with your life, then you should not adopt them as yours own. This goes for all areas of your life; health, relationship, family, friendship, etc. In life, no one has the same two standards. You might have similar standard as other people, but they are not the same.

If your standards are lower than other people in certain areas, then that does not mean your standards are bad, and it definitely does not mean you have to change yours to meet other people standards. It does not mean other people are better or smarter than you when they have higher standards. If you try to reach other people standards, it means you are trying to impress them.

When you are working toward your own standards, they will be easy and enjoyable for you in order to accomplish things. Sometimes it might take you awhile to reach your standards of success or happiness, but they will be pleasant journeys.

If you have a difficult time reaching your success or happiness standards in any area of your life, then try applying the following action steps:

ACTION STEPS

1. Write down every area of your life

2. Write down what does success look and feel like to you in each area. For example, what does success and happiness in health mean to you? What does success and happiness in relationship mean to you?

3. For each area, do you have a difficult time reaching or moving forward in your level of success and

happiness? If you are having trouble, then it means you are trying to accomplish someone else standard.

4. For each area that you are having a difficult time with, think and write down where did that standard come from? How did you come up with that standard? Where did you read it from? Where did you watch it from? Who did you hear it from? Where did you learn it from?

5. Create a new standard for yourself. If one standard does not work, keep on finding a standard that match your life. Do not give up.

Quality vs. Quantity

Have you ever encountered moments when you feel like you have done so many things, but somehow, you still feel unsatisfied or something is still missing from your life?

If you answer yes to the question, then there are two main reasons why. First, you have been doing things that do not bring you happiness. It does not matter how much effect you put into doing the wrong things; they will never bring you happiness. For example, if you do not like to play football, then it does not matter how much effect you try to like football, you are not going to like football. In this case, you want to make sure you are doing things that will bring you happiness.

Second, you want to make sure you give things time to develop and grow before you can experience enough happiness. Most things require you to reach a certain level before happiness can manifest. If you stop before you reach the happiness level, then you are not going to experience happiness. Also, happiness is something that you have to keep on pursuing. For example, if playing tennis brings you happiness, then you have to keep on playing in order to maintain that happiness. Playing tennis one time will only bring you happiness at that moment. There is no destination for happiness. Happiness is an ongoing process that requires constant actions. The more actions you take, the happier you will become.

"Happiness is found in doing, not merely possessing."

Napoleon Hill

(Author of "The Law of Success")

If you ever feel unsatisfied with your accomplishments, then try to think back on how many action steps you took? Did it take you a few steps or many? And how much effect did the steps take for the accomplishments to occur?

You might accomplished many things, but if you did not take many steps to accomplish them, then your happiness would not be as high compared to another person who accomplished fewer things, but took many steps with a higher effect level to achieve their goals. For example, when you are working on a project, it is the hard work and the feelings that you develop throughout the process that determine your happiness, and not the outcome of the project. It is the same when you work on challenging problems. The main reason why challenging problems will bring you more happiness than simple problems is because they require you to put more time and effect into them.

"Success is a journey, not a destination. The doing is often more important than the outcome."

Arthur Ashe

(3 Times Tennis Grand Slam titles)

Another example is when you fall in love with someone. When you first met them, you would not know if you love or even like that person or not, right? It is only after you get to know and understand that person then your love beings to develop for that person. The more you understand that person, the more appreciation it will grow, which will translate into love.

In this case, the majority of your happiness is based on quality, not quantity. The wonderful thing is that whatever and whoever is already in your life, they will bring you happiness if you give them time to grow.

If you are not experiencing happiness from what you are doing in your life, then try applying the following action steps:

ACTION STEPS

1. List down every aspect of your life (personal, private, public, health, career, relationship, etc.)

2. For each area, write down every single thing that you would need or want to do in order to bring you

happiness. For example, if your children are a part of your life, then list down everything you would need to do for them such as: taking them to school, feeding them, bathing them, or reading them bedtime stories. Or your health such as: exercising, eating, sleeping, mentality, spirituality, etc. You want to list down every signal thing for each area.

3. Look through all of your life areas, and only pick out the top 3 tasks that are the most important to you. If you could only do 3 tasks out of everything on your life, what would your top 3 be?

4. For each of your top 3 tasks, what is your goal for each one? For example, if you say exercise is one of the top 3, then what is your goal for exercising in your life? Is it 3 times per week, or 1 time per week, or every day? Or if you say reading a bedtime story to your child is important, then what is your goal? Is it reading to them every day, once a week, three times a week, or whatever you set your goal to be? To make your goals even better, you want to be as specific as possible. For example, how long will your

exercises be, 30 minutes, 60 minutes, or 2 hours? Or if your goal is to read to your children, is it for 30 minutes, 60 minutes, or 2 hours?

5. You want to make sure you do not fail and most important keep on improving on your top 3 goals. The 3 goals, you want to make sure you accomplish them no matter what happen. The better you accomplish your 3 goals, the happier you will become. Your top 3 goals are like your 3 daily tasks for your job. If you do not accomplish your top 3 tasks for your job, then you will be fired. In this case, if you do not accomplish your top 3 daily goals, you will suffer a lot. For example, if your goal is to exercise 3 times per week, you want to make sure you accomplish that goal. Furthermore, the more you improve on your exercise routines for the 3 times per week, the happier you will become.

6. For each of your goal, you want to research and discover the benefits that will manifest if you are able to accomplish your goals perfectly. For example, if you are able to feed your children with

the best nutrition, what are the positive outcomes for your children? Or if your goal is to exercise, what are the positive outcomes if you are able to exercise perfectly? And that is what you what to aim for. You want to be the best you can for your top 3 goals. It is like reaching for the stars. Even though you cannot be perfect on your top 3 goals, you still want to be the best you can be on them.

Moving Forward

"If you can't fly, then run. If you can't run, then walk. If you can't walk, then crawl. But whatever you do, you have to keep moving forward."

Martin Luther King Jr.

(American activist, humanitarian, and leader of the African-American Civil Rights Movement)

Do you sometimes stop yourself from moving forward to improve your life because you believe that where you are at in life is already good enough? Do you believe that you would be happier staying where you are at than trying something new?

If you answer yes to at least one of the questions, then it means that you have stopped seeking for happiness. From the chapters on "True Happiness" and "Gratification vs. Happiness," happiness is not based on things, results, or destinations to be reached, but based on how high your inner strength, courage, and self-development are through taking actions that will help those qualities grow. The moment those qualities stop on growing, the moment your happiness stop on growing.

The main reason why you have to keep on moving forward as a human being to grow your strength, courage, and self is because you are a living thing. Living things have to either grow or die; they do not stay the same. For example, a tree is a living thing. It either dies or grows. It never stays the same. The tree might be 100% alive today, but if you do not water it tomorrow, its life span will decrease to 99%. Even though 99% is still great, it is still dying. If you do not water the tree for two days in a row, then it will decrease down to 98% of its lifespan. When you do not water your tree at all, it will become dead.

You also have to keep on growing to increase your courage, strength, and self in order to keep your happiness strong. Otherwise, you will also die slowly from the inside, and then it will transform to the outside of yourself. It does not matter where you are in life; you have to keep on moving forward.

"If we don't change, we don't grow. If we don't grow, we aren't really living."

Gail Sheehy

(Author of "Passages" and "New Passages")

"It may be alright to be content with what you have, but never with what you are."

Fitness Motivator

(A fitness website to help you be and stay fit)

You need to believe that it is never too late to grow and move forward in life to experience happiness. For example, let's say that you are 90 years old, and you believe that it is too late for you to do anything to improve your life because you are too old already. However, if someone gives you one million dollars the next day, would you take it at the age of 90? Of course you would right? You know that one million dollars will help you become a happier person because you do not have to worry about financial issues anymore and you can do whatever you like. In this case, you would accept the one million dollars at the age of 90 because you know it will increase your happiness; even though you only have a short amount of time left to live. In this case, it is the same with happiness. It is never too late to increase your courage, strength, and self in order to grow and experience happiness. Even though you only have 5 or 10 years left of your life, you would rather experience the last 5 or 10 years of happiness and not at all.

"It is never too late – never too late to start over, never too late to be happy."

Jane Fonda

(American writer and fitness guru)

If you have trouble moving forward in life, then try applying the following action steps:

ACTION STEPS

1. Write down everything in your life that you want to improve and grow

2. For each one individually, write down at least two things on how you can improve and keep on moving forward in that area

3. Write down new things that you would like to learn and accomplish

4. For each new thing, research the steps on how to get there

5. Take action right away

Extra: Self-Esteem Quotes

"Why are you trying so hard to fit in when you were born to stand out?"

Fitness Motivator

"Happiness is really a deep harmonious inner satisfaction and approval."

Francis Wilshire

"Always be a first-rate version of yourself, instead of a second-rate version of somebody else."

Judy Garland

"Never apologize for showing feeling. When you do so, you apologize the truth."

Benjamin Disraeli

"Follow your bliss and the universe wills open doors for you where there were only walls."

Joseph Campbell

"You are an ocean knowledge hidden in a dew drop."

Jalaluddin Rum

"Knowing is not enough, we must apply. Wishing is not enough, we must do."

Johann Von Goethe

"In every negative event is the seed of an equal of greater benefit."

Napoleon Hill

"We are not independent but inter-dependent."

Thich Nhat Hanh

"You gain strength, courage and confidence by every experience in which you really stop to look fear in the face."

Eleanor Roosevelt

"There is no failure – just experience and your reactions to them."

Thomas Krause

The moment you start changing to please people, you will be taking a step backward."

Joel Osteen

"I will change when I wish or need to change, when the moment for change is ripe. Until then I will remain as I am."

Stacey Charter

"Be yourself, everyone else is already taken."

Oscar Wilde

"Be careful the friends you choose for you will become like them."

W. Clement Stone

"Having one good friend is worth more than being popular amongst many."

Carolynn Warner

"You train people how to treat you by how you treat yourself."

Martin Rutte

"The way you treat yourself sets the standard for others."

Sonya Friedman

"People laugh at me because I am different, I laugh at them because they are all the same."

Swami Vivekananad

"**There is only one person who could ever make you happy, and that person is you.**"

David Burns

"**It is not easy to find happiness in ourselves, and it is not possible to find it elsewhere.**"

Agnes Repplier

"**No one outside ourselves can rule us inwardly. When we know this, we become free.**"

Thich Nhat Hanh

"**Nothing can bring you happiness but yourself.**"

Ralph Waldo Emerson

"What lies behind us and what lies before us are tiny matters compared to what lies within us."

Ralph Waldo Emerson

"When there is no enemy within, the enemies outside cannot hurt you."
African Proverb

"If people believe in themselves, it's amazing what they can accomplish."
Sam Walton

"Indecision is the thief of opportunities."

Jim Rohn

"If you can't fly, then run. If you can't run, then walk. If you can't walk, then crawl. But whatever you do, you have to keep moving forward."

Martin Luther King Jr.

"Inside of every problem lies an opportunity."

Robert Kiyosaki

"Trust your hunches. They're usually based on facts filed away just below the conscious level."

Dr. Joyce Brothers

"Self-trust is the first secret of success."

Ralph Waldo Emerson

"You have something to offer this world that nobody else does! You have incredible talents and gifts to share with others."

Joel Osteen

"All of us do not have equal talent, but all of us should have an equal opportunity to develop our talents."

John F Kennedy

"The world has the habit of making room for the man whose actions show that he knows where he is going."

Napoleon Hill

"My life is my message."

Mahatma Ghandi

"To fulfill your destiny, stay tune to your heart. Don't let anyone squeeze you into a mold."

Joel Osteen

"Always remember that you are absolutely unique. Just like everyone else."

Margaret Mead

"Happy people are those who feel truly terrific about themselves and this is the natural outgrowth of accepting responsibility for their life."

Brian Tracy

"You make the world a better place by making yourself a
better person."

Scotto Sorrell

"Trust yourself. You know more than you think you do."

Benjamin Spock

"If we don't change, we don't grow. If we don't grow, we
aren't really living."

Gail Sheeh

"Confidence comes not from always being right but from
not fearing to be wrong."

Peter T. Mcintyre

**"When you have confidence, you can have a lot of fun.
And when you have fun, you can do amazing things."**

Joe Namath

"Just as much as we see in others we have in ourselves."

William Hazlitt

**"Nothing builds self-esteem and self-confidence like
accomplishment."**

Thomas Carlyle

**"To be yourself in a world that is constantly trying to
make you something else is the greatest
accomplishment."**

Ralph Waldo Emerson

"It is better to be hated for what you are than to be loved for what you are not."

Andre Gide

"We learn by doing."

Aristotle

"Doubt can only be removed by action."

Johann von Goethe

"When you follow the dream in your heart, you're energized, inspired, and motivated."

Dr. John F. Demartini

"It is better to be alone than in bad company."

George Washington

"It is never too late – never too late to start over, never too late to be happy."

Jane Fonda

"You need to make a commitment, and once you make it, then life will give you some answers."

Les Brown

"When you find peace within yourself, you become the kind of person who can live at peace with others."

Peace Pilgrim

"Action is the foundation key to all success."

Pablo Picasso

"Why try and to be fake when being real takes less effort."

Inspirational Quotes

"Put your future in good hand ---- your own"

Mark Victor Hansen

"Once you make a decision, the universe conspires to make it happen."

Ralph Waldo Emerson

About Mykim Tran

Mykim Tran is a self-esteem expert, motivational speaker, trainer, and life coach. Her mission in life is to help transform individuals in order for them to create and live the lifestyle they love through believing and using their own inner strength and talent.

In 2008, Mykim started the process of self-development in order to learn as much as possible about herself and where true happiness comes from. She would spend times on reading, listening to audios, and watching DVDs on self-development and self-help materials such as happiness, success, self-esteem and self-confidence.

Through applying the techniques she learned on personal development and taking good care of herself physically, mentally, and spiritually, she was able to create and live the life that she loves. You can learn more about Mykim at www.mykimtran.com.

Be yourself and live your life as *YOU*

Mykim Tran's Workshops and Programs

Self-Esteem Building: Live your life as YOU

If you enjoy and benefit from this book, then this is your chance to attend the live workshop. Come and experience firsthand on how you can take your knowledge and turn it into real life experiences. Come unleash your power from within to be yourself. Learn how to block out external influences to make your own decisions. Learn how to attract the right people into your life. Learn how to find true happiness and fulfillment and create and live the lifestyle as YOU.

Be in control of your life: Live the life you love

Do you have a difficult time keeping your life in balanced and control? Do you feel unsatisfied and unappreciated in your life? Are you not enjoying life anymore? Do you have difficult times accomplishing your daily tasks and responsibilities? Do you want to get things done faster? Do you have high level of stress? Do you want to develop a balanced and fulfilling lifestyle?

If you answer yes to at least one of the questions, then this workshop is for you! Come learn how to develop a balanced and fulfilling lifestyle so you can live the life you love.

Maximum Health

Do you know how much you need to eat to keep your body energized and hydrated? Do you always worry if you are eating or exercising enough, too little, or too much for your body? Do you always struggle to exercise? Do you have a difficult time waking up in the morning feeling refresh? Do you believe staying healthy is too much work?

If you answer yes to at least one of the questions, then this workshop is for you! Come learn how to create step-by-step plan to unleash your energy and health.

Goal setting support group

Do you have trouble accomplish things in life? Do you set goals and end up not doing anything about them? Do you tend to procrastinate and not get anywhere with your goals?

If you answer yes to any of the questions, then this Goal Setting Support Group is for you. Come learn how to develop and set goals that will bring you success, fulfillment, and happiness. Come learn how to stay motivated to become successful.

Monthly Interaction

- Weekly support group

- Motivational challenges

- One-on-one coaching

- Unlimited emailing to coach

- And so much more!

Lifestyle Coaching Program

Are you confused on what you should be doing in your life? Are you lost in life? Do you feel you have done so many things, but not getting anywhere in life? Do you need more focus? Do you want to accomplish your dreams and goals? Are you lack in motivation?

If you answer yes to any of the question, then this coaching program is for you.

Learn how to increase energy and decrease stress. Increase self-confidence and self-esteem. Learn how to develop and maintain a healthy and fulfilling lifestyle. Unleash inner strength and talent and passion/life purpose. Learn how to enjoy life more. Increase physical, mental, and spiritual wellness.

Wake-Up package

If you are ready to create and live the lifestyle that is filled with energy, joy, and purpose, then this Wake-Up package is for you. This package includes all three workshops: Self-Esteem Building, Be in Control of Your Life, Maximum Health, one year membership subscription to the Goal Setting Support Group, and 3 months of lifestyle coaching.

If you would like to learn more about the workshops and programs, please log on to www.wake-upfoundation.org